COOL CAREERS WITHOUT COLLEGE FOR
PEOPLE
WHO LOVE
CRAFTS

COOL CAREERS WITHOUT COLLEGE FOR PEOPLE WHO LOVE CRAFTS

STEPHANIE MANNINO

The Rosen Publishing Group, Inc.
New York

Published in 2004 by The Rosen Publishing Group, Inc.
29 East 21st Street, New York, NY 10010

First Edition

Library of Congress Cataloging-in-Publication Data

Mannino, Stephanie.
Cool careers without college for people who love crafts/
by Stephanie Mannino.
    p. cm. — (Cool careers without college)
Includes bibliographical references and index.
ISBN 0-8239-3785-2
1. Handicraft—Vocational guidance. I. Title. II. Series.
TT149 .M33 2002
745.5'023—dc21
                               2002011808

Manufactured in the United States of America

CONTENTS

INTRODUCTION

If you enjoy dabbling in crafts but have only considered crafts as a hobby, take heart—you may be able to earn a living making things that you love. Many people create and sell their crafts. The types of crafts they make, their artistry and skill, and where they sell their products helps dictate what they earn. Dollar for dollar, what you earn will depend on the cost of your materials and the time you spend creating your craft.

To turn your hobby into a career, you will have to work very hard and be extremely dedicated. Among many considerations will be whether to sell your creations wholesale (to someone who will mark up the price and sell it to the public), or retail (to someone who will use it). This is a decision that will affect your profits.

To learn more about the possibilities of a career in crafts, attend classes, read books, and talk to professionals in the field. Linda Powers, president of the Arts and Crafts Association of America, told the author that trade shows sponsor classes and certification opportunities. Major cities and surrounding areas offer a wide range of arts and crafts shows, art festivals, and art galleries. The leading states for arts and crafts are Florida, California, Colorado, Arizona, Ohio, Michigan, New York, and Pennsylvania.

If a career in crafts is what you see in your future, explore the possibilities now. Many types of people decide to go into the arts and crafts business. As Powers says, "You have professional artists and crafters who decide to make a career out of what they love doing, and you also have the leisure crafter. Any age can enjoy crafts, and it is not gender-specific. Most everyone has a creative side." She adds, "Since most artists and crafters are independents and run their own business, students should prepare themselves with not only art classes, but business classes as well."

The arts and crafts industry earns $14 billion annually and continues to grow each year. This book describes many careers in crafts and what it takes to succeed in the craft business. If you love to express your creative side, the time is always right to explore the possibilities of a cool career in crafts.

FOR MORE INFORMATION

ORGANIZATION

Arts and Crafts Association of America (ACAA)
4888 Cannon Woods Court
Belmont, MI 49306
(616) 874-1721
Web site: http://www.artsandcraftsassoc.com
The ACAA is a national organization that supports independent artists and crafters throughout the United States. The long-range plan of the board of directors is to develop chapters in each state.

BASKET MAKER

Basket weaving is thought to be one of the world's earliest crafts. Archaeologists have suggested that people may have developed the technique of weaving baskets from the methods that they used for weaving shelters from tree branches.

Description

Basket weavers need a great sense of touch. Good hand-eye coordination is also essential. Creating a basket can take hours, days, or weeks, so it is important that the basket maker be patient and able to stick to the task at hand.

Baskets can be made out of many materials. Once chosen, the materials are either coiled or woven to form the basket. Reeds, splint, and wild vines, which tend to be long and sturdy, are usually woven. Shorter materials, such as pine needles and grass, are coiled because they are more delicate.

There are dozens of basket types that you can create using weaving or coiling techniques. A type of woven basket that has maintained its popularity over the years is the elegant Shaker basket. Named for a religious group in the United States that made these baskets until 1925, this classic beauty is now made by many basket weavers.

Education and Training

Sharon Dugan, a basket maker from New Hampshire, became interested in making baskets when she was a child in the 1950s. She learned to make her first baskets from her mother.

"When I discovered ash splint and Shaker baskets, I took lessons from a local elderly basket maker," says Dugan. "After learning the basics from her, I obtained a job working for a nationally known Shaker basket maker." Before the basket making company agreed to take Dugan on as an

A basket maker weaves a basket from lygodium (a Japanese climbing fern) and rattan. Basket making can be painstaking work, but many people find it relaxing.

employee, they wanted to see that she had the skills to be a basket maker. "I got the job by showing them some of my baskets," says Dugan

According to Dugan, the best way to learn basket making is to take classes. She suggests following introductory training by making baskets from commercial kits. "Once you are familiar with materials and techniques, you can create your own work," she says. Check with your local community college, adult education programs, or basket shops to see what classes are available.

The craft of basketry is not limited to highly skilled craftspeople. According to Dugan, "Anyone, including small children, can master simple basket weaving." If you have the desire to learn, begin by making simple baskets. As your skill develops, you may be able to turn your interest into a life-long career.

Salary

Most basket makers work independently so their earnings vary greatly. A company that does hire basket makers is the Longaberger Basket Company in Newark, Ohio. According to Helene Meyer, executive director of the National Basketry Organization, Inc., basket makers earn about $30,000 per year. People who teach basket making also earn approximately $30,000 annually. Basket prices can range from $45 for a small willow creation, to several thousand dollars (though this is rare) for an intricate, sculptural design.

Outlook

Many craftspeople sell their work for retail prices at craft fairs, on the Internet, or from their studios. Most basket makers either follow traditional techniques or create their own unique styles.

If you become highly skilled and are a good communicator, you may want to consider teaching. According to Dugan,

A basket maker instructs junior high school students in the art of weaving baskets. As with most crafts, basketry requires a lot of practice once one has learned the basics of the craft.

"A number of basket makers earn their living by traveling around the country teaching at basket conventions, seminars, and craft schools.

"I sell most of my baskets directly to collectors, followed by fine craft shops and galleries, and lastly, online," says Dugan. "I do one nine-day craft fair a year. It's the League of New Hampshire's Annual Craftsmen's Fair in August." The first of its kind in the nation, this highly respected event is known for having only the best of the best in fine arts and crafts. "It takes me all year to make enough baskets to sell at the fair, to supply the league shops, the Canterbury Shaker Village Museum store, and select galleries, and fill custom orders," says Dugan.

Dugan's advice for future basket makers is simple: "Persistence, persistence, persistence. The person who persists will succeed in the end. And as long as there are customers who value the fine craft of handmade baskets, you'll be able to find a market for your products."

Profile

Sharon Dugan, Basket Maker

THE BEST ASPECTS OF HER JOB

For Sharon Dugan, working at home in her own studio has its advantages. "My work environment is on a farm in a pleasant, light-filled, two-car garage with nice windows. I try to work there each weekday from about 7 AM to 4 or 5 PM. I like working at my own pace, producing beautiful objects, creating and experimenting."

WHAT DOES SHARON LIKE THE LEAST ABOUT HER JOB?

"That's easy!" she says. "Demands on my time. Folks sometimes find it hard to realize you're working when you are 'at home.'"

As a one-person business, the biggest challenge is to have enough time to produce the product. "I wear many hats and have to run all the errands," says Dugan.

FOR MORE INFORMATION

RECOMMENDATIONS FROM SHARON DUGAN

Rosen, Wendy W. *Crafting as a Business*. New York: Sterling Publishing Company, Inc., 1998.

Gratiot Lake Basketry
Star Route 1, Box 16
Mohawk, MI 49950
(906) 337-5116
e-mail: glbasketry@worldnet.ATT.NET
Web site: http://www.gratiotlakebasketry.com
A good source for materials and kits.

ORGANIZATIONS

The Agassiz Harrison Fibre Arts Group
Box 383
Harrison Hot Springs, BC VOM 1K0
Canada
e-mail: lscobie@uniserve.com
Most members weave traditional willow baskets. Regular workshops are held for members and others interested in traditional crafts.

The Basketry Network
1850 Bloor Street East, Suite 106
Mississauga, ON L4X IT3
Canada

Greater Vancouver Basket Weavers

(604) 469-0840

Part of the Greater Vancouver Weavers and Spinners Guild, this group meets the first Monday of each month. The members take turns hosting these meetings.

National Basketry Organization, Inc.

P.O. Box 681

Mercer, WI 54547

(715) 360-8519

e-mail: nbobaskets@centurytel.net

Web site: http://www.nationalbasketry.org

A not-for-profit educational group that provides a wide range of information about the art of basketry. Its Web site includes a forum, membership form, Web links, and more.

Nova Scotia Basketry Guild

121 Crichton Avenue

Dartmouth, NS B3R 3R6

Canada

(902) 469-2798

e-mail: joleen.gordon@ns.sympatico.ca

WEB SITES

Baskets, Etc.

http://www.bright.net/~basketc/

A site for the exchange of information about making splint, reed, and willow baskets.

BasketMakers.org

http://basketmakers.org

A good source of information, this site offers *Spoke 'n Weaver*, a free basketry newsletter.

COMPANIES

The Longaberger Company
1500 East Main Street
Newark, OH 43055
(740) 322-5900
Web site: http://www.longaberger.com
This quality basket company has a reputation for putting people first.

BOOKS

Cary, Mara. *Basic Baskets*. Boston: Houghton Mifflin, 1975.

Gillooly, Maryanne. *Natural Baskets: Create Over 20 Unique Baskets with Materials Gathered in Gardens, Fields, and Woods*. Pownal, VT: Storey Communications, 1992.

Johnson, Kay. *Basketmaking*. London: Batsford, 1991.

Meilach, Dona Z. *A Modern Approach to Basketry with Fibers and Grasses, Using Coiling, Twining, Weaving, Macramé, Crocheting*. New York: Crown Publishers, 1974.

Pollock, Polly. *Basketmaking: Get Started in a New Craft with Easy-to-Follow Projects for Beginners*. Edison, NJ: Chartwell Books, 1994.

Siler, Lyn. *The Basket Book*. New York: Sterling, 1988.

Wright, Dorothy. *The Complete Book of Baskets And Basketry*. 3rd ed. New York: David & Charles; Distributed by Sterling Pub. Co., 1992.

PERIODICALS

The Crafts Report
100 Rogers Road
P.O. Box 1992
Wilmington, DE 19899-9776
(800) 777-7098
Web site: http://www.craftsreport.com
This business magazine for craft professionals features surveys and industry information.

BOOKBINDER

Since paperback binding arrived on the scene about fifty years ago, there has been a decrease in the quality of bound books. Enter the book-binder: a person who is dedicated to the pursuit of the high standards with which books were once bound.

Description

Over years, books are subject to wear-and-tear caused by many factors,

A bookbinder decorates a leatherbound book with gold leaf at the Folger Shakespeare Library in Washington, D.C. The process of blocking includes stamping letters into leather bindings.

including repeated use, rough handling, climate, and age. Treasured family heirlooms, such as family bibles or irreplaceable editions of important works of literature, including first editions of rare books, often need to be repaired at some point, especially if they are very old.

Denis Gouey, a bookbinder in Torrington, Connecticut, specializes in restoring books and in the preservation of important documents, photos, and artwork. A typical day for Gouey starts around 8:00 AM and ends from 6:30 to 7:00 PM. He says, "Light is essential, so well-lit rooms are the perfect situation for a bookbinding studio. My work environment is different than most binderies because of the storefront. I operate as a book/print/art shop. Of course, there is the

Interview with Denis Gouey, Bookbinder

Denis Gouey fell in love with books at an early age. "When I was a kid, my mother took me to the market every Saturday where there was a seller with used books displayed on a table. I became fascinated with books and all the paraphernalia around them: the people, the stories, the knowledge, and the beauty."

In high school, Gouey applied for a printing program at a trade school, but the career advisor thought he'd be better at bookbinding because of his artistic talent. It was good advice. "Emphasis was bench work, but also history and art. I did well. The class was small and the teacher terrific, and at seventeen-and-a half years old I graduated and soon found my first job."

Gouey finds bookbinding to be a rewarding and fulfilling career. "Being instrumental in the creation or preservation of historical objects brings on a sense of great satisfaction. The interaction with objects and clients is a rewarding experience. It makes for a very interesting life."

Internet business, answering mail, and other tasks, and I do this after work hours."

Education and Training

Gouey thinks that someone who wants to learn bookbinding should find a good bookbinding school. "There are only a few schools where one would learn basics of the trade. Keep in mind that it requires a long time and a lot of practice to master this trade. If school is not an option," says Gouey, "there are bookbinding guilds in most states. Start with a basic program, and buy instructive books on both the history and the practice of bookbinding." It is also helpful—but not always necessary—to be knowledgeable in the areas of art, art history, basic geometry, chemistry, calculus, time management, and communication, Gouey says.

While there is a lot to learn about bookbinding, Gouey feels that anyone gifted with good hand-eye coordination has the aptitude for it. "The skills are acquired with practice," says Gouey. He also says that a person must be imaginative and able to solve problems from start to finish. "Patience and artistic curiosity are only some of the needed virtues of the successful

A bookbinder prepares to use a needle and thread to attach the pages of a book to the cover.

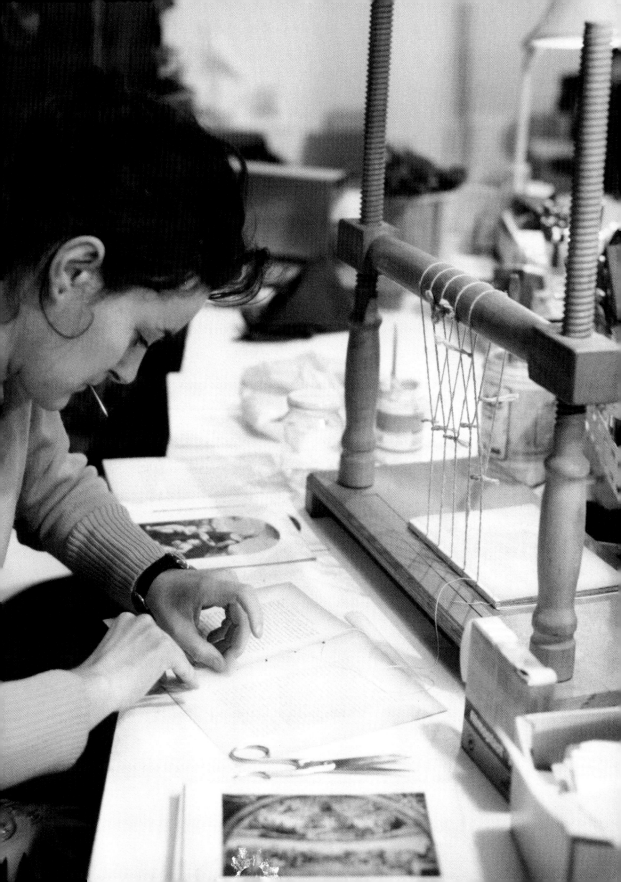

Forwarding and Finishing

Forwarding is the process of assembling a book. It includes folding the leaves of paper into pages and sewing them together. It also involves constructing the cover and attaching the pages and endpapers to it. Finishing refers to embellishing the cover with the book's title and decoration. Finishing can include tooling the cover, or adding inlays, onlays, or any other technique the bookbinder chooses.

bookbinder, along with good ethical values, respect for the past, open-mindedness, and thirst for learning," says Gouey.

Denis has advice for students considering bookbinding careers: "Stick with simple but traditional structures. Make sure you understand the principles of a sound binding. Buy some books on the topics. Join a discussion group on the Internet."

Salary

Gouey has found that bookbinders are paid for the work they produce on a variety of scales. For instance, university or bindery departments usually offer about $22,000 as a yearly salary. A bindery supervisor can make around $50,000 per year. "Salaries for bench work in private binderies are less at the start, but can develop into a better and different salary scale. This is especially true if the employee is gifted," says Gouey. Benchwork is focused on the physical aspects of binding, including disbinding, repairing, assembling, sewing, and covering. It had been done by old time journeymen.

A bookbinder in private practice is compensated in direct proportion to his or her skills. Binding prices vary between $100 and several thousand dollars per unit. Binders who command several thousand dollars for individual pieces are rare and are usually masters of their craft.

Outlook

A bookbinder can find work in binderies, at universities, and at libraries. A bookbinder can also be self-employed. Being close to a major metropolitan area is an advantage for a bookbinder and can result in larger commissions. But, says Gouey "Good bookbinding can be done everywhere. The most important advertising tool is word of mouth. If one is gifted, the word goes around quickly."

In some ways, the outlook for bookbinding as a career is uncertain. Print-on-demand, says Gouey, "is very much a product of the Internet and my definition of it is simply photocopying rare or otherwise unobtainable books that are no longer copyrighted or are in the public domain." He adds that it is a growing business with out-of-print book dealers. "I believe that publishing will come to this in the future, thus cutting the printing cost, waste and all, getting closer to a more ecologically friendly industry," says Denis.

FOR MORE INFORMATION

ORGANIZATIONS

American Institute for Conservation of Historic and Artistic Works (AIC)
1717 K Street NW, Suite 200
Washington, DC 20006
(202) 452-9545
Web site: http://aic.stanford.edu

The Canadian Bookbinders and Book Artists Guild (CBBAG)
176 John Street, Suite 309
Toronto, ON M5T 1X5
Canada
(416) 581-1071
e-mail: cbbag@web.net
Web site: http://www.cbbag.ca
The Canadian Bookbinders and Book Artists Guild has provided support for the development of book arts since 1983.

Center for Book Arts
28 West 27th Street
New York, NY 10001
(212) 481-0295
e-mail: info@centerforbookarts.org
Web site: http://www.centerforbookarts.org
The goal of the Center for Book Arts is to preserve traditional bookmaking techniques as well as to encourage people to create books as contemporary art objects.

Guild of Book Workers (GBW)
521 Fifth Avenue
New York, NY 10175
Web site: http://palimpsest.stanford.edu/byorg/gbw/

SCHOOLS

American Academy of Bookbinding
P.O. Box 1590
135 S. Spruce Street
Telluride, CO 81435
(970) 728-3886
Web site: http://www.ahhaa.org/AAB.html
Both professional binders and motivated students can receive top-notch instruction through eight weeks of intensive binding courses from May through mid-July.

Columbia College Chicago Center for Book and Paper Arts
1104 S. Wabash, Suite 200
Chicago, IL 60605
(312) 344-6630
e-mail: bookandpaper@popmail.colum.edu
Web site: http://www.colum.edu/centers/bpa

Nebraska Book Arts Center
University of Nebraska at Omaha
60th and Dodge Streets
Weber Fine Arts Room 124
Omaha, NE 68182-0173
(402) 554-2773
Web site: http://www.unomaha.edu/~nbac/home.html
The Nebraska Board of Regents founded this organization in 1989 to support appreciation of books and promote artful book production.

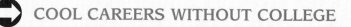

North Bennet Street School
39 North Bennet Street
Boston, MA 02113
(617) 227-0155
e-mail: nbss@nbss.org
Web site: http://www.nbss.org
Begun in 1986, this is the only full-time bench bookbinding program in the United States. Classes in this two year course of study run from September to June for six students a year.

WEB SITES

Bookbinding and the Conservation of Books
http://palimpsest.stanford.edu/don/don.html
A dictionary of bookbinding terms by Matt T. Roberts and Don Etherington. Illustrations are by Margaret R. Brown.

BOOKS

Banister, Manly Miles. *The Craft of Bookbinding*. Mineola, NY: Dover Publications, Inc., 1993

Barrett, John Paul. *How to Make a Book: An Illustrated Guide To Making Books by Hand*. Astoria, OR: Gaff Press, 1993.

Fox, Gabrielle. *The Essential Guide to Making Handmade Books*. Cincinnati, OH: North Light Books, 2000.

Kropper, Jean G. *Handmade Books and Cards*. Worcester, MA: Davis Publications, 1997.

Lavender, Kenneth. *Book Repair: A How-To-Do-It Manual*. 2nd ed. New York: Neal-Schuman Publishers, 2001.

McCarthy, Mary. *Making Books by Hand: A Step-By-Step Guide*. Rockport, MA: Quarry Books, 1997.

3

CALLIGRAPHER

Calligraphy, a French term meaning "beautiful writing," is an art form known for its distinctive style of lettering. For many centuries, calligraphers in Islamic countries, Japan, India, and China have worked with a brush.

Calligraphy as we know it in the Western world began with early cave paintings that were abstract images. The Egyptians by

Especially with calligraphy, practice makes perfect! Here, a calligraphy student uses a flat nibbed pen to fill page after page with calligraphic letters.

about 3500 BC had created pictures that represented important events. They used these pictures, called hieroglyphics, to keep records on papyrus paper and to cover the walls of tombs.

By 850 BC, the Romans had developed a kind of writing with which to record their language, Latin. By the Middle Ages, Latin had become the language of Europe's churches. Monks painstakingly transcribed ancient text into beautifully lettered and illustrated books.

The invention of the printing press in the mid-1400s made it faster and less expensive to produce books. But the printing press was too awkward for everyday correspondence and invitations. Calligraphy flourished!

Description

A calligrapher creates attractive lettering on documents that usually have special significance. Think of the last time you saw the envelope for a wedding invitation or a diploma written with beautiful, flowing lettering. Because each letter is created by hand, it is a slow, painstaking process. It is not a good career choice for an impatient person. However, if you have the artistic talent and tenacity to study and practice this art form, calligraphy can be extremely rewarding.

People hire calligraphers because they want their documents, invitations, or other printed pieces to stand out and have a distinguished appearance. A calligrapher may work on his or her own, in a self-owned business, or perhaps provide services through a larger graphics company.

Calligraphy can help to create a special mood of joy, elegance, and importance. The hand lettering of calligraphy can make the smallest details—such as place cards at a wedding—even more special.

Education and Training

"The best education comes from hands-on doing and learning," says Richard Tuttle, publications director for

Calligraphy: Then and Now

With the invention of the typewriter in 1867, beautiful penmanship became less important. In the twentieth century, devotees of calligraphy created a renewed interest in the craft. While visiting the United States in 1974, Donald Jackson, a well-known English calligrapher, promoted the art of calligraphy through lectures and workshops. He also did television interviews during his visit, encouraging Americans to form their own calligraphy societies. His enthusiasm for the art caught on. Today there are more than thirty calligraphic societies in the United States and Europe.

the Association for the Calligraphic Arts. "If one wants to pursue this as a career option, it would be best to find a good instructor. Or, if possible, more than one, since instructors differ slightly from one another." He advises to "take as many classes as possible over a period of time. And practice, practice, practice! From there, find a way to become an apprentice, which will continue the hands-on learning process."

Salary

What a calligrapher earns depends on the project and the client. "Payment can range from ten dollars for making a little bookmark to many thousands of dollars for creating a one-of-a-kind art piece," says Tuttle.

Outlook

Print shops, craft stores, schools, colleges, and publishers hire calligraphers. As Tuttle reports, "One of the biggest employers of calligraphers in the U.S. would have to be greeting card companies, like American Greetings. Card companies usually attend a yearly international conference just for job recruiting."

The job rate for calligraphers has steadily grown over the past few years. But, cautions Tuttle, that doesn't mean someone is ready to become a professional calligrapher with only a little practice. "Sometimes the local area is flooded with individuals who feel they can offer calligraphy services after taking one course or learning from a book." People who set themselves up as professionals too soon actually end up hurting the field.

There seems to be more of a demand for calligraphy in larger cities and neighboring areas. But, Tuttle adds, "Calligraphers can find work just about anywhere as long as they look."

Working conditions are as varied as the types of projects that calligraphers can create. A calligrapher can be self-employed, work in a corporate environment, or work in the White House, penning invitations to special events or for awards. For people interested in pursuing a career in calligraphy, Richard thinks that it is also important to be interested in art.

FOR MORE INFORMATION

ORGANIZATIONS
Association for the Calligraphic Arts
1223 Woodward Avenue
South Bend, IN 46616
(574) 233-6233
e-mail: aca@calligraphicarts.org
Web site: http://www.calligraphicarts.org
This nonprofit organization was founded in 1997 to raise awareness of calligraphy and help people learn this beautiful art. It sponsors publications, special programs, exhibits, and other activities.

Calligraphy Societies of Florida
Web site: http://www.calligraphers.com/florida
The calligraphy guilds of Florida have joined forces to promote the lettering arts in their state. Meeting at least once a year, the societies sponsor an annual weekend retreat and publish a newsletter.

The Calligraphy Society of Ottawa
P.O. Box 4265
Station "E"
Ottawa, ON K1S 5B3
Canada
(613) 747-0795
e-mail: jgregoir@magma.ca
Web site: http://www.ncf.ca/cso
With a membership of nearly 100 people, this society attracts professionals as well as observers.

Society for Calligraphy
P.O. Box 64174
Los Angeles, CA 90064-0174
(213) 931-6146
e-mail: linderander@earthlink.net
Promoting appreciation of calligraphy as a fine art, this not-for-profit organization has about 1,000 members, making it one of the world's largest calligraphy societies.

Washington Calligraphers Guild
P.O. Box 3688
Merrifield, VA 22116
(301) 897-8637
e-mail: info@calligraphersguild.org
Web site: http://www.calligraphersguild.org
The Washington Calligraphers Guild, founded in 1976, is a nonprofit organization with approximately 500 American and international lettering artists. From beginners to professionals, members appreciate calligraphy and book arts.

BOOKS
Couch, Malcolm. *Creative Calligraphy: The Art of Beautiful Writing.* London: Tiger Books International, 1996.

Gray, Jim. *Brush Lettering Step by Step*. Cincinnati, OH: North Light Books, 2001.

Hufton, Susan. *Calligraphy Project Book: A Complete Step-by-Step Guide.* New York: Sterling Publishing Company, 1995.

Marsh, Don. *Calligraphy.* Cincinnati, OH: North Light Books, 1996.

Nash, John. *Practical Calligraphy*. New York: Smithmark, 1992.

CERAMIST
AND POTTER

Do you like to use your hands to mold forms from soft, pliable clay? Do you like to experiment with shapes and colors? Do you like to make three-dimensional objects that you can use for drinking your morning coffee or for displaying flowers? Perhaps you are already a sculptor who thrives on creating one-of-a-kind designs. Earning a living with the plastic arts may be just for you!

Ceramics artist Jeremy Bundick molds a bowl of clay as it turns on the potter's wheel. He must apply the right amount of pressure to the clay to produce a bowl that is even, straight, and free of flaws.

Description

Clay is a natural material that can be found along banks of streams and rivers. Natural clay is available in many colors, including white, ivory, yellow, gray, red, blue, and black. However, professional ceramists and potters buy clay that has been cleaned of pebbles and grit. The clay is mixed with other ingredients to make it suitable for commercial use.

The difference between ceramics and pottery is the surface of the finished object. Porcelain and stoneware, which are hard and extremely durable after being fired in a kiln (a special oven that reaches very high temperatures) are ceramic. Earthenware, which is softer and much more porous when fired, is pottery. Nearly all ceramic or earthenware creations must be coated with glaze and fired again (at least once) to decorate and seal the surfaces. Glazes can be transparent, opaque, clear, or colored. They can be used to create a variety of surfaces, from dull to shiny.

Before beginning a project, the ceramist must knead the clay to eliminate air bubbles trapped inside. The ceramist checks the clay for air bubbles by cutting through it. If the clay contains even tiny imperfections, it can fall apart or explode under the stress of firing.

Ceramists and potters can fashion many items out of clay, including mugs, plates, jars, pots, bowls, and vases. People who earn their living from their pottery usually design and craft their own distinct lines of products.

Some ceramists and potters produce their designs in volume, while others specialize in one-of-a-kind pieces. Ceramists and potters sell their work from their workshops, in stores, or at craft shows and fairs.

Some people build their designs by hand, while others fashion them on a potter's wheel. Using the potter's wheel may look easy and its products can be beautiful, but it takes a lot of practice to master it.

Ceramists and potters work in studios, either in their homes or in shared spaces. Either way, a studio is an area

A Syracuse China kiln operator moves unfinished ceramic plates into a kiln at the company's plant in Syracuse, New York. The kiln is a kind of oven used to fire, or harden, clay.

fitted with worktables, a kiln, and many other kinds of equipment. It may not always be necessary to own all the equipment, but for the professional it certainly helps.

Education and Training

People interested in trying their hand at ceramics or pottery have several options. They can check with local community colleges for classes. Four-year colleges and universities sometimes offer evening classes for the general public through continuing education programs.

People do not need to be full-time students in the school to take these continuing education classes, but they benefit from the college's faculty and equipment when they study there.

Community arts organizations offer classes in ceramics and pottery, as do neighborhood ceramic studios and high schools with adult education programs. These organizations may also run intensive ceramic or pottery programs during the summer.

Types of Clay

Earthenware clay is opaque and slightly porous. It is sometimes white and sometimes has color. When people talk about pottery, they're often referring to earthenware.

Stoneware is nonporous and stronger than earthenware. Because stoneware must be fired at extremely high temperatures, its colors are subdued.

Porcelain clay, which is white, is also stronger than earthenware. When fired, thin porcelain is delicate and translucent. It has the finest texture of the three types of clay. Expensive china is made from porcelain.

Salary

According to the *Crafts Report*'s 1999 Insight Survey, people working in ceramics earned an average of approximately $37,000 per year.

Outlook

Selling your wares at craft markets and fairs or shops are just some of the ways to earn money with ceramics. You may have noticed that shops where customers can paint and decorate pre-sculpted pottery have been popping up all over the place. Opening a studio like this is one way to expand your career in ceramics. Another way to earn money with ceramics is to teach. You're not alone in your interest in ceramics, and once you've mastered the craft, there will certainly be others willing to learn from an experienced ceramist.

FOR MORE INFORMATION

ORGANIZATIONS
FUSION: The Ontario Clay & Glass Association
Cedar Ridge Creative Centre
225 Confederation Drive
Toronto, ON M1G 1B2

Canada
(416) 438-8946
e-mail: 2fusion@interlog.com
Web site: http://www.clayandglass.on.ca
This nonprofit is the only arts organization in Ontario dedicated to helping creators and collectors of handmade clay and glass. Members include artists, teachers, collectors, guilds, libraries, and international businesses.

BOOKS

Arima, Elaine, Kevin Nierman, and Curtis H. Arima (illustrator). *The Kids 'N' Clay Ceramics Book: Handbuilding and Wheel-Throwing Projects from the Kids 'N' Clay Pottery Studio*. Berkeley, CA: Tricycle Press, 2000.

Hart, Anne Button, and Doris W. Taylor. *Creative Ceramics for the Beginner: Step by Step*. Princeton, NJ: Van Nostrand, 1968.

Savage, George. *An Illustrated Dictionary of Ceramics: Defining 3,054 Terms Relating to Wares, Materials, Processes, Styles, Patterns, and Shapes from Antiquity to the Present Day*. New York: Thames and Hudson, 1985.

Techniques of the World's Great Masters of Pottery and Ceramics. Edison, NJ: Chartwell Books Ltd., 1997.

Triplett, Kathy. *Handbuilt Tableware: Making Distinctive Plates, Bowls, Mugs, Teapots, and More*. New York: Lark Books, 2001.

PERIODICALS

Ceramics Monthly
735 Ceramic Place
Westerville, OH 43086-6102
(614) 794-5890
Web site: http://www.ceramicsmonthly.com
This is an international magazine about ceramic art and crafts.

Clay Times
15481 Second Street
P.O. Box 365
Waterford, VA 20197
(800) 356-CLAY (2529)
(540) 882-3576
e-mail: CLAYTIMES@aol.com
Web sites: http://www.claytimes.com
Clay Times is a magazine that provides international news about events and exhibits related to clay. It also offers practical information about creating art with clay.

DECORATIVE PAINTER

Decorative painting has been around in one form or another for thousands of years, beginning, perhaps, with cave people who painted on walls. Decorative painting can be applied to many kinds of surfaces, from floors, to walls, to furniture, to signs.

Description

Craft painting can take on many forms. Painted decorations on preexisting

A San Juan sign painter adds the finishing touch to an advertising sign bearing an image of the Puerto Rican flag.

objects, such as walls, cabinets, chairs, and frames, is one way to create unique-looking, special pieces.

Many sign painters still design and paint letters and graphic designs by hand on many kinds of signs. You've probably seen some of their work, including window signs and billboards. If you've ever seen the name of a business or person painted on a glass door, that's the work of a sign painter who used a brush and paint. A skilled sign painter can run a successful small business, or a sign painter can find employment with a graphics company or a company specializing in outdoor advertising.

Stenciling, a technique used to decorate a surface with paint, has recently experienced a surge in popularity. Far from a new craft, stenciling dates as far back as 2500 BC, when it was used by Egyptians. Other cultures also incorporated stenciling as an art form, although its exact origin is unknown.

A popular craft in colonial America, today, stencils are used to decorate furniture, walls, boxes, paper, fabric, and many other surfaces. Visiting a stencil shop, or the stencil department of an art or craft supply store, will give you an idea of the variety of stencil patterns available. You may even get to take a practice lesson, as many stencil stores provide classes.

Once a stencil design has been cut out of stencil paper, the artist uses a stencil brush, a sponge, or a roller to apply the design to the wall or other surface. A stencil artist can

Painting on Glass

Use acrylic enamel paint to decorate small glass objects, such as drinking glasses, plates, or vases, with designs, sayings, or images. To make your designs permanent, bake the glass for half an hour in an oven at 350 degrees Fahrenheit.

A member of the Baltimore Ravens grounds crew adds the finishing touches to the team's logo at midfield in Memorial Stadium.

move much more quickly than a painter who works free-hand, because the stenciler uses the same design over and over again. Using fast-drying acrylic paints will simplify the process for you.

Education and Training

There are many traditional faux, or fake, finishes to learn to paint as well as a variety of decorative styles including French country, trompe l'oeil (meaning "fool the eye"), as well as early American. It's a good idea to begin by taking classes in the areas that interest you, advises Janelle Johnson, teacher services and education director of the Society of Decorative Painters. "Find a class and start to paint in your spare time."

"You should have lots of self-discipline and have good people skills," says Mary M. Wiseman, president of the Society of Decorative Painters, who has been involved in decorative painting for twenty-five years. "You should have a drive and incentive in all aspects of the career."

Salary

Mary M. Wiseman reminds prospective decorative painters that they won't earn a huge income in the beginning. "It's a difficult field. Be patient and have long-range goals. It's very competitive, and you should not expect a lot of money."

Wiseman has seen decorative painters earn from $15,000 to $25,000 a year, depending on the individual. The type of work that you do and how often you work will determine your income.

Outlook

Decorative painting is a creative endeavor, and most painters work alone. A drawback can be that self-employed decorative painters have no benefits. You may also have to

Murals

A mural is a type of painting that can be created on a grand scale. Often seen on the exteriors of buildings or interior walls, murals tend to be much larger than traditional paintings that hang in homes. Murals can add a dynamic color statement to the outside of a building or create an important point of interest or mood within a room.

Before beginning to paint, the mural artist designs an image to fit the scale of the project. Once the wall has been cleaned, sealed, and primed, the painter transfers the image onto the wall. The artist can work with a grid, with a projector that throws an image of the drawing on to the wall, or freehand.

Fresco painting is a type of mural technique which is created on freshly spread, moist, lime plaster walls. For this, the painter makes a cartoon (a full-scale drawing), fastens it to the wall, and presses the outlines into the plaster wall. The artist uses the outlines as a guide when applying the paint. In fresco painting, the paint is made from powdered pigments that are mixed with water.

work evenings and weekends. There are companies, however, that specialize in decorating furniture so it is possible to get a full-time job.

Teaching is a wonderful way to help others learn the craft while keeping your own skills fresh. In addition, decorative painters often branch out into other fields. Many have become art product salespeople, designers, authors of instructional books, and demonstrators at craft shows or fairs.

FOR MORE INFORMATION

WEB SITES

Faux Like a Pro.com
http://www.fauxlikeapro.com
This site provides detailed information about decorative finishes, including instructions. There's also an online store selling professional-grade supplies.

Folkart.net
http://folkart.net/
A Canadian source for locating teachers of decorative painting and supplies, and other helpful information.

Murals Plus
http://www.muralsplus.com
Check here for inspiration or help painting murals, faux finishes, stencilling, or other forms of wall decorations.

PERIODICALS

Paintworks Magazine
All American Crafts, Inc.
243 Newton-Sparta Road
Newton, NJ 07860
(973) 383-8080
Web site: http://www.paintworksmag.com

VIDEOS

Color Blending
Shows what can be painted; how to prepare a surface; what primer or base coat to use; how to choose colors; how to mix paint to the correct consistency for wall painting; and how to use tissue paper, feathers, erasers, rags, washes, and more.

Gilding, Crackle, Patina
Demonstrates faux painting and furniture refinishing techniques that can be applied to most surfaces. Includes information about leaving, woodgraining, crackle, and patinas.

Marbleizing, Ragging, Faux Decorative Painting and Furniture Refinishing Techniques
This tape explains explains various techniques for decorative painting and furniture refinishing.

Murals Made EZ
This two-and-a-half hour tape shows you how to paint murals. It includes step-by-step instructions.

Stencils and Strokes
For experienced stencilers who want to expand their skills in mixing and applying paint.

Trompe L'oeil
Learn to use light and shadow to create architectural images that trick the eye.

All videos are available from:
Golden Brush
68733 Perez Road, Suite C10
Cathedral City, CA 92234
(888) 774-3222
e-mail: info@fauxvideos.com

FLORAL DESIGNER

If you enjoy the colors, shapes, textures, and delicacy of flowers, perhaps floral design is for you. Arranging flowers in vases is just one of the many possibilities within a floral design career. You can also use flowers to make wreaths, potpourri, centerpieces, bouquets, and hair accessories. Floral designers are not limited to using real flowers,

Florists who design for special occasions need to know what flowers work well together and when they are in season.

either—silk flowers also make lovely decorative pieces. Dried flower arrangements are another way to create from flowers.

Description

Flowers have long been considered the ultimate gift for showing appreciation and love. Think of how many flowers are delivered to people each year on holidays, birthdays, and anniversaries! Because flowers continue to hold sentimental value for so many people, the floral industry offers many opportunities.

Elements of Floral Design

In addition to flowers, there are three basic elements that go into constructing an arrangement: the container, the plant material, and the mechanical aids. Understanding these three items is one of the first steps to learning basic floral design.

Containers

Choosing the right container to hold an arrangement is not always easy. A floral designer must keep in mind what the design will look like and choose the container that will best compliment the color, texture, and proportion of the arrangement.

Plant Material

In creating flower arrangements, the designer usually uses fresh flowers or plants, although silk or dried flowers and plants can also be used. Most floral designers purchase their materials from wholesale suppliers.

Mechanics

A base or armature is usually placed inside the vase or container to hold the flower stems in place. Neat, clean, and unobtrusive floral foam and chicken wire are often used. The most popular way to hold plants in place is with a needle holder or pin holder (sometimes called a kensan). Good needle holders are straight-sided with a heavy lead base and an abundance of sharp, pointed, and closely spaced needles.

Designers often construct the foundation of the design by lining and filling a container. They use fresh plant material, decorative wood, or even wire, plastic, or rope. Filler plants, which have small blooms, serve as a background for the main flowers in the arrangement. Baby's breath is often used as filler.

Education and Training

If you are interested in working in the floral industry, you can start out as an employee in a flower shop. Learning on the job is one possibility. But you can also begin by taking classes. Look in the catalogs of local trade schools, vocational schools, community colleges, and botanical gardens for classes in floriculture or horticulture.

Knowing a lot about design is certainly necessary, but running a successful business will present many of its own challenges. If you plan to open your own business, learn as much as you can about small business management and marketing.

A master floral designer teaches a student the traditional Japanese art of flower arranging at an agricultural high school in Mobara, Japan.

Salary

Salary varies within the floral industry, depending on whether a designer works full- or part-time, alone, or for a large company. According to a private college study performed by the Craft Organization Directors Association (CODA), professional crafters on average make between $23,000 and $32,000 annually, but this is a broad figure that covers many other industries besides floral design.

Outlook

The floral industry appears to prosper under every economic condition. People always seem to want flowers to celebrate marriages, graduations, and birthdays. People also use flowers at funerals and other solemn occasions. Each year, about $12 billion worth of flowers are sold in the United States. This adds up to a lot of business for floral designers.

Some floral designers start their own businesses, while others work in flower shops. Floral design can be a very rewarding and satisfying career, although it does have the disadvantage of being seasonal. During certain times of the year business may be very busy, with people working long hours. Celebrations such as Valentine's Day and Mother's Day are especially busy times for florists and floral designers.

FOR MORE INFORMATION

ORGANIZATIONS
American Floral Endowment
11 Glen-Ed Professional Park
Glen Carbon, IL 62034
(618) 692-0045
e-mail: afe@endowment.org
Web site: http://www.endowment.org

According to its Web site, "The American Floral Endowment funds research and educational development in floriculture and environmental horticulture." Designed to "produce solutions to industry needs and promote the growth and improvement of the floral industry," the research benefits the grower; wholesale, retail, and allied businesses; as well as the general public.

Society of American Florists (SAF)

1601 Duke Street
Alexandria, VA 22314
(800) 336-4743
Web site: http://www.aboutflowers.com
A national trade association for the floral industry, this society represents growers, importers, wholesalers, and retailers of flowers and plants.

SCHOOLS

Algonquin College

1385 Woodroffe Avenue
Nepean, ON K2G 1V8
Canada
(800) 565-4723
(613) 727-0002
Web site: http://www.algonquinc.on.ca
This one-year certificate program provides students with the skills necessary to succeed in the floral industry. Courses cover all aspects of caring for, handling, displaying, and selling flowers and plants.

American Institute of Floral Designers

720 Light Street
Baltimore, MD 21230
(410) 752-3318
e-mail: AIFD@assnhqtrs.com
Web site: http://www.aifd.org
According to its Web site, "the American Institute of Floral Designers was established in 1965" by a small group of leading floral designers

dedicated to recognizing and promoting "the art of floral design as a professional career." They are "committed to establishing and maintaining higher standards in professional floral design."

Rittners School of Floral Design
345 Marlborough Street
Boston, MA 02115
(617) 267-3824
e-mail: Stevrt@tiac.net
Web site: http://www.floralschool.com

Seneca College of Applied Arts and Technology, Retail Florist Program
1750 Finch Avenue
East Toronto, ON M2J 2X5
Canada
(416) 491-5050
Web site: http://www.senecac.on.ca/fulltime/REF.html
Graduates are prepared to work as floral designers, sales consultants and advisors, and management trainees in all branches of the flower industry.

WEB SITES

Flora Source
http://flora-source.com
(888) 883-5672
e-mail: info@flora-sour
A site packed with great information, including online job postings for all segments of the floral industry.

Floral Home Company's Wholesale Links and Resources for the Floral Trade
http://www.floralhome.com/linksflo.htm

7

GLASSMAKER AND GLASSBLOWER

For people who are artistically as well as technically inclined, glassmaking and glassblowing can be enormously exciting. They are crafts that require three-dimensional talents, as well as a feel for shape, color, and texture.

Description

Glass dates back to somewhere after 2500 BC. Some of the oldest

A glassblower stretches a piece of hot molten glass by swirling it during the blowing process.

examples of glass, including beads, amulets, and vases, have been found in the tombs of Egyptian pharaohs.

In its earliest form, glass was made by melting a combination of silica and alkali. Through the generations, other substances have been used to improve the quality of the glass. Today glass is made by heating a chemical called flux, mixed with sand and an alkali, in a crucible (a heat-resistant container) at approximately 2,500 to 2,700 degrees Fahrenheit. After the mixture has melted, the furnace is turned down, letting the glass cool to 1,800 degrees Fahrenheit.

A Brief History of Glassmaking in the United States

Glassmaking has been around since prehistoric times. The first glass objects were made from natural glasses such as obsidian (volcanic glass) or rock crystal.

The first glass factory in the United States was built in 1608, and glass was carried in the first cargo exported to England. Caspar Wistar, a German-born manufacturer, set up the first successful large-scale glasshouse in 1739 in New Jersey. Manufacturer H. W. Stiegel, who was also German-born, produced some of the finest colonial glassware in his Pennsylvania glasshouses.

An American named Deming Jarves invented a glass-pressing machine around 1827. It was used in his Boston and Sandwich Glass Company. The glass-pressing machine introduced mass-produced glass products. But glassmakers were still able to earn a living making glass the old-fashioned way, even as the country embraced mass-produced glass. Fine craftsmanship was still highly valued.

Louis C. Tiffany, an American artist, designed and manufactured an iridescent glass used in a variety of art objects in the late 1800s. Sidney Waugh is another American artist known for creating exceptionally fine blown glassware.

In the contemporary world, glass is used in modern architecture to transmit electricity; as an instrument in scientific research; and for lighting, optical instruments, household utensils, and even fabrics. New forms of glass have revolutionized the industry. Safety glass, which is usually constructed of two pieces of plate glass bonded together with a plastic that prevents the glass from shattering when broken, is one of the modern innovations in glass technology. However, there still remains a place for the craftsperson who uses glass to create objects of beauty. The unique pieces created by craftspeople offer something much more special than mass-produced objects.

If the glassmaker wishes to create an object by blowing glass, he or she shapes a glob of molten hot glass on the end of a pontil, or long metal blowpipe. The glassmaker blows into the pipe, creating a bubble from the molten glass that adheres to the end of the pipe. When the glassmaker is satisfied with the size of the bubble, he or she shapes the hot glass with tools while twirling the glob to counteract the pull of gravity.

Master glass artist Dale Chihuly *(right)* demonstrates the glassblowing process to a group of students at a workshop in Tacoma, Washington.

Education and Training

It may be difficult to find classes in glassblowing. Check local schools or colleges, especially those that specialize in fine or industrial art. If you know of a local glassmaker or glassblower, ask to become an apprentice. You might also ask glassmakers how they got started in the field and if they would recommend any programs or classes in your area. In addition, glassblowing schools offer instructional courses on the Web with supplementary videotapes.

Glassblowers and glassmakers need a lot of patience, dexterity, and precision. If you are a perfectionist, glass-making may be an appropriate field for you. Also, you must be able to tolerate exposure to intense heat, which is part of the process.

Salary

Glass artisans can earn a good living. The *Crafts Report's* 1999 Insight Survey reported that those who work with glass earned an average of $46,500 per year.

Outlook

Glassblowing is a difficult and highly specialized craft. It takes a tremendous amount of determination and practice to learn. But those who master glassblowing hold very creative jobs. Some glassblowers work alone in their own businesses. Others are employed in factories, producing glassware, decorative items, or glass for science and industry. Some glassblowers teach their craft to beginners.

FOR MORE INFORMATION

ORGANIZATIONS

Creative Glass Center of America

1501 Glasstown Road
Millville, NJ 08332-1566
(800) 998-4552
(856) 825-6800, Ext. 2733
e-mail: cgca@wheatonvillage.org
Web site: http://www.creativeglasscenter.com
Located in historic Wheaton Village is the Museum of American Glass, a folk life center, the T.C. Wheaton Glass factory, and a stained glass studio. Wheaton Village offers craft demonstrations, artist fellowships, outreach programs, and more. Its goal is to educate people about the role of crafts, yesterday and today.

FUSION: The Ontario Clay & Glass Association

Cedar Ridge Creative Centre
225 Confederation Drive
Toronto, ON M1G 1B2
Canada
(416) 438-8946
e-mail: 2fusion@interlog.com
Web site: http://www.clayandglass.on.ca
This not-for-profit organization is the only Ontario arts organization for people who collect and craft handmade clay and glass. Members include artists, students, teachers, guilds, collectors, libraries, hobbyists, and international businesses.

The Glass Art Association of Canada
P.O. Box 475
Saltspring Island, BC V8K 2W1
Canada
e-mail: jgoodman@saltspring.com
Web site: http://acsa.corp.eol.ca/aboutg.html
A volunteer, member-run organization offering Canadian glassmakers, students, and collectors a communication network through the publication of their quarterly journal, the *Gazette*.

International Guild of Glass Artists
27829 365th Avenue
Platte, SD 57369
(313) 886-0099
Web site: http://www.igga.org
Dedicated to "facilitating communication among and between glass artists for the promotion and encouragement of excellence in the glass arts." Produces a quarterly newsletter, *Common Ground: Glass*, and publishes a yearly industry source guide. Open to all stained glass artists.

International Society of Glass Beadmakers
1120 Chester Avenue #470
Cleveland, OH 44114
(888) 742-0242
Web site: http://www.isgb.org

The National American Glass Club, Ltd.
P.O. Box 1497
Hagerstown, MD 21741-1497
e-mail: nagc@att.net
Web site: http://www.glassclub.org
This nonprofit, international organization is designed for people who study and appreciate glass of all types, periods, or origins.

Public Glass
1750 Armstrong Avenue
San Francisco, CA 94124
(415) 671-4916
Web site: http://www.publicglass.org
Public Glass is a nonprofit center for creating art glass. It offers classes at all levels in glass blowing, casting, and flame work. Artists may rent work space.

UrbanGlass
647 Fulton Street
Brooklyn, NY 11217
(718) 625-3685
Web site: http://www.urbanglass.org
Founded in 1977, UrbanGlass is a not-for-profit center where artists can rent studios and take classes. Lessons are available for beginners as well. About 900 people study at UrbanGlass each year. In addition to programs abroad, the Bead Project, and the Bead Expo, UrbanGlass offers some courses for college credit.

BOOKS

Flavell, Ray, and Claude Smale. *Studio Glassmaking*. New York: Van Nostrand Reinhold Co., 1974.

Schuler, Frederic. *Glassforming: Glassmaking for the Craftsman*. Philadelphia: Chilton Book Co., 1970.

PERIODICALS

Glass Line Newsletter
Web site: http://www.hotglass.com
A newsletter for hot glass artists. Founded April 16, 1987.

8

LEATHER CRAFTER

Despite the increased use of synthetic and manmade materials, leather products are still valued for their durability and beauty. Leather artisans can create unique, carefully crafted products, which many people value.

Description

Leather products are made from the skin or hide of animals. Cowhide,

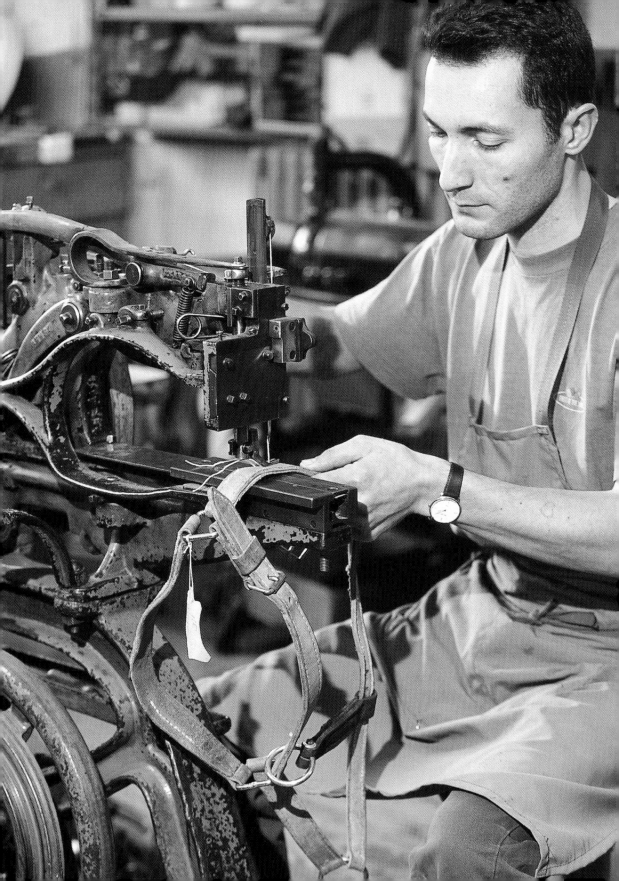

which is abundant, is used most frequently. Leather artisans also use goatskin, pigskin, calfskin, sheepskin, and steer hide. Leather has many uses—as clothing, shoes, belts, hats, furniture, and even sculpture. The potential for leather products is almost limitless.

There are two main types of leather markets: commercial trade and custom leather. Commercial trade includes mass-produced and primarily machine-made items, such as belts, wallets, leather clothes, and furniture. A person in this field will probably work for a large manufacturer.

Custom leather products and art leather are primarily handcrafted, but the leather artisan might use a machine for some of the work. Custom work is sold at craft fairs, craft shops, galleries, and by commission.

Education and Training

Thom Keach, president, founder, and lifetime member of the International Internet Leathercrafters Guild (http://www.iilg.org) advises those interested in leather craft to "take high school or college classes in art, design, color, and even some marketing, since much of your work

A leather artisan uses a machine to repair a leather strap. Some artisans repair leather by hand-sewing.

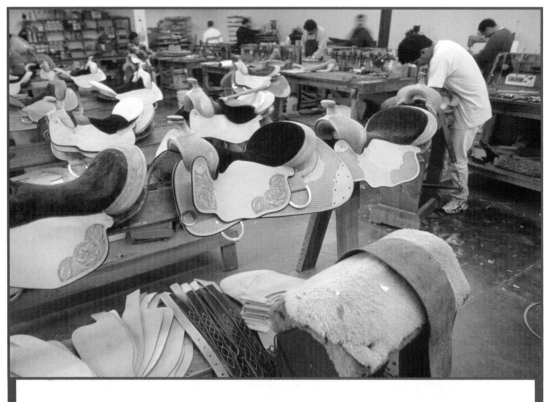

Factory workers making saddles by hand in a leather-craft factory

may be sold to individuals. Also try to find a local leather artist to teach or mentor you. Consider joining a local leather guild in your area or join the IILG."

"For a person who is wanting to learn leather craft, I would suggest that they explore whether there is anyone in their immediate area who is doing leatherwork," says renowned leather crafter Ron Ross. "They might check with a local tack shop to see if the operators know of anyone doing leather carving. Then I would suggest that they contact that person to see if they would be interested in taking on a student."

Love Your Work

For more than fifteen years, Wayne Christensen has created carved custom leather products as part of his business, Leather by WC, in Reseda, California. "I get to do what I love and get paid for it," says Wayne, about the best part of his job.

Salary

"Leather workers will probably start at minimum wage and move up the pay scale as they gain skill and experience," says Keach. "On the custom side, each individual leather artist is free to determine his or her hourly rate and the price of their own work. A custom-made saddle can sell for thousands of dollars, as can a large leather art piece." According to the *Crafts Report's* 1999 Insight Survey, people who sold leather crafts earned an average of $28,167 per year.

Outlook

The outlook for a career in leather craft is good; Keach points out that as long as people want products made from leather there will be companies that mass-produce goods and individual leather artists making one-of-a-kind items. Probably the most in-demand pieces are leather saddles, as well as belts, wallets, purses, and shoes.

Types of Leather Designs

Tooling

Leather artisans create a variety of designs using tools to compress the surface of the leather. They rub the tools, which may have pointed, balled, or flat ends, over damp leather to create a pattern, texture, or design.

Stamping

Another way to create a design is by stamping the leather with a copper pipe or filed large-headed nails. A leather artisan uses a mallet to press a stamp into damp leather. The artisan must be careful that the leather is just wet enough—leather that is either too wet or too dry will not hold the impression of the stamp.

Carving

Moist, natural cowhide, calfskin, or sheepskin are the best choices of leather for carving. In the simplest form of carving, the artisan uses a swivel knife to cut designs into the leather and a flat, modular tool to press the background. Leather artisans develop unique styles of carving since there are few rules to follow when decorating the leather with this technique.

Profile

Ron Ross is saddle maker, leather artist, and member of the IILG. His interest in leather, which began when he was very young, has lasted for nearly forty-five years. Since leaving the army as a young adult, Ross has followed a career in leather both part- and full-time.

"My specialty now is carving in the style called Sheridan," reports Ross. He wrote his first book, East of Sheridan, *as a result of people wanting to learn his Sheridan style of carving. A clamor for additional patterns resulted in his writing a second book,* Sheridan Designs.

Ross is also a saddle maker. "Early on, in the early 1960s, I started to do saddle repair for myself and for others. This eventually evolved into the making of saddles. I must classify making of saddles as one of my favorite phases of leatherworking." His work also includes driving harnesses, workhorse harnesses, and saddles, both plain and fancy.

Ross has a 450-square-foot shop at his home on a farm on the main highway between two small towns, St. Joe and Spencerville, Indiana. "My philosophy is, when I have work to do, I do it." He also sells his work online via his Web site.

"The person who wants to pursue leatherwork as a career must first be dedicated to learning all that they can to perfect their skills," says Ross. "They must constantly strive

to improve their work, and to excel. They must also be willing to often work long hours for a low wage or return on their investment. Often, the satisfaction of having done a job well must suffice for the low wage or profit that they might make in the beginning."

FOR MORE INFORMATION

ORGANIZATIONS

Canadian Society for Creative Leathercraft
264 Duke Street, Suite 401
Hamilton, ON L8P 1Y3
Canada

Colorado Saddle Makers Association
P.O. Box 385
Franktown, CO 80116
Web site: http://www.coloradosaddlemakers.org
CSMA is a nonprofit organization that represents Colorado's professional saddle makers. It aims to encourage the tradition of handmade western saddles. It provides educational programs and encourages communication between saddle makers.

The Honourable Cordwainers' Company
Web site: http://www.thehcc.org
This organization works to preserve the skills, techniques, and traditions of boot and shoe making, and associated trades. It has a growing international membership of men and women.

International Internet Leather Crafter's Guild

Web site: http://www.iilg.org

This guild uses the Internet to bring together leather workers from around the world. It aims to promote the art and craft of leather by helping people share ideas and information.

O-MI-O Leathercraft Guild

(810) 984-3228

e-mail: cjbleather@advnet.net

A group of leather crafters from Michigan, Ohio, and Ontario.

Tandy Leather Company

5882 E. Berry Street

Fort Worth, TX 76119

(888) 890-1611

e-mail: tlc@tandyleather.com

Web site: http://www.tandyleather.com

Tandy Leather has long been the resource of leather crafters. It offers quality tools, leather accessories, kits, and teaching resources.

WEB SITES

The Honourable Cordwainers' Company

http://www.thehcc.org

International Internet Leather Guild

http://iilg.org

PERIODICALS

The Leather Crafters and Saddlers Journal

331 Annette Court

Rhinelander, WI 54501-2902

(888) 289-6409

(715) 362-5393

e-mail: journal@newnorth.net

Written for the leather crafting community, this is the only publication for the craft. Endorsed by the IILG.

VIDEO

Carving Leather

Featuring Bob Dellis, professional leather carver, in a set of ten carving videos teaching viewers how to carve leather. See the IILG Web site (http://www.iilg.org) for ordering information.

9

NEEDLE-WORKER

Needleworkers use thread or yarn to stitch on cloth or mesh to make pillows, quilts, wall hangings, and chair covers, as well as decorating and fashion accessories.

Description

Needlework stitchery covers a wide range of styles and techniques. One style is called crewel embroidery. Stitched with wool or silk thread on linen, silk, or wool fabric,

Knitting requires a lot of patience and attention to the number of stitches in each sequence. Over time, knitting becomes second nature to experts. In the end, seeing the completed project is often reward enough for experts and amateurs alike.

crewel embroidery usually depicts traditional designs that include leaves and flowers.

Needlepoint is a style of stitchery in which wool yarn completely covers a canvas mesh. The finished piece, which is exceptionally strong, is appropriate to use as upholstery, handbags, picture frames, rugs, and slippers. One style of needlepoint is Bargello, distinguished by bold, elegant geometric patterns. Needlepointers can stitch intricate designs depicting flowers and scenery by working on a tiny mesh called petit point. Skilled needlepoint designers can create custom designs for clients, depicting family members, pets, or other personal images.

One way to dress up any fabric is to add beadwork. With this method of needlework, a waxed thread and needle are used to cross-stitch beads onto material or canvas. A bead-worker can cover an entire item with beads to produce a striking finished product.

Knitting is yet another form of needlework. Using yarn and needles, a knitter can create an array of useful and artistic items including sweaters, scarves, hats, or afghan blankets to sell at craft fairs or shops.

Handmade items can last for years and make wonderful gifts.

Education and Training

To learn to do a specific type of needlework, take a class at a craft shop or through an adult education program. Once you're comfortable with a technique you can buy your own equipment (needles, canvas, and a frame if necessary) and experiment with different styles, designs, and stitches. Books are also a great source of information for the beginner. Look for books with lots of descriptive diagrams and explanations.

Be patient when learning needlework, and start small! Large projects can be overwhelming to a beginner. As you progress, the quality and complexity of your pieces will improve.

A Short History of Needlework

Egyptian embroidery is visible in tomb paintings that show decorated clothing and hangings. The Romans, who called it "painting with thread," held needlework in high regard. Basic needlework stitches probably haven't changed much over centuries, although the needles are

A display of traditional embroidery in a shop window in Szentendre, Hungary

much different. Ancient people probably used bone, wood, or ivory to sew warm, simple clothes from animal skins. Today, needles are made of plastic or steel.

Needlework was also used to adorn garments worn by clergymen during the Middle Ages. The embroidery was stitched by monks and nuns.

The embroidery on the traditional clothing in Russia and central Europe reflected where a person was from. Homemakers embroidered many household items, embellishing curtains, bedspreads, and towels.

Needlework was very popular in America during colonial times. Learning to stitch was part of a girl's education, and she often created a cross-stitched sampler. A vehicle for practicing stitches and learning to read and write, samplers often featured numbers, letters, poetry, and prayers, as well as flowers, buildings, and animal motifs. Many samplers hang in historical societies and museums today, reminders of the beauty and durability of embroidery.

Outlook

Needleworkers sell their products at craft fairs, shows, and galleries. There are also artist cooperatives where needleworkers (as well as other craft artisans) can sell their creations. Some needleworkers are so skilled that they can earn a living by creating customized items to customers' specifications or by producing works of art.

FOR MORE INFORMATION

ORGANIZATIONS

American Needlepoint Guild, Inc.
P.O. Box 1027
Cordova, TN 38088-1027
(901) 755-3728
Web site: http://www.needlepoint.org
The American Needlepoint Guild, Inc. (ANG), is an educational, nonprofit organization for amateur and professional, novice and experienced stitchers.

Craftsmen's Studio
2778 Tabernacle Church Road
Pleasant Garden, NC 27313
e-mail: email@craftsmensstudio.com
Their e-mail newsletter furnishes educational information, designer profiles, special sales, and more.

The Embroiderers' Guild of America, Inc.
335 West Broadway, Suite 100
Louisville, KY 40202
(502) 589-6956
e-mail: EGAHQ@aol.com
Web site: http://www.egausa.org
The goal of this guild is to preserve and promote the highest standards of traditional embroidery.

Web Sites

Counted Cross Stitch, Needlework, and Stitchery Page
http://www.dnai.com/~kdyer

Embroiderers' Association of Canada
http://www.islandnet.com/embroidery/homepage.html
This association promotes the art of embroidery in its many forms. Its Web site links to local chapters, youth programs, correspondence courses, and more.

International Council of Needlework Associations (ICNA)
http://www.geocities.com/nonprof01/ICNA/icna.htm
Formed in September 1990, this council works to promote the art of needlework. It also provides resource information.

The Needlework Designers of Canada
http://www.headachesolvers.com/needle/index2.htm
This organization seeks to help new and established designers promote their work. Its newsletter links members throughout Canada.

BOOKS

Dillmont, Thérèse de. *The Complete Encyclopedia of Needlework*. 3rd ed. Philadelphia: Running Press, 1996.

Elder, Karen. *Embroidery*. New York: Clarkson Potter, 1995.

Nichol, Gloria. *Cross Stitch*. New York: Clarkson Potter, 1995.

PICTURE
FRAMER

Family photographs and special pieces of artwork often need one thing to make them complete: a frame. And what better way to preserve and protect those special pictures than to have them framed by a professional? Perhaps you have a few pictures you've been thinking of framing, or maybe you've wondered what it takes to frame them yourself.

A frame maker carefully applies fragile gold leaf, also called gilt, to the surface of a frame.

Description

There is more to the craft of picture framing than popping a photo into a store-bought frame. In addition to being patient, artistic, and enthusiastic, a picture framer needs a deep appreciation for the many elements that combine for attractive and protective framing of photographs, works of art, or other important items. Framers enjoy working with their hands and eyes, and suggesting framing options to customers who want to display and protect their diplomas, needlework, certificates, and rare documents. Being able to judge proportion, as well as coordinate color, texture, and proportion, are vital to the success of a framer.

Picture framers assemble frames by cutting and assembling molding. They choose the color and texture of mat board and cut mats, or windows, to border and protect the pictures inside the frame. A picture framer must be mindful of how the image to be framed will relate to its surrounding.

Framers cut glass and "fit" all the elements cleanly into the frame. In addition to preserving the art, a frame and mat should enhance it as well as the area where it hangs.

Education and Training

The Professional Picture Framers Association (PPFA) advises students to take workshops and classes offered at industry trade shows. These usually last just a few days.

There are framing schools that give basic courses as well. If you're unable to locate a place that offers formal instruction, reading books about picture framing and practicing at home is another option.

In order to gain experience, a novice picture framer might consider finding a part-time job in a picture framing

A picture framer researches materials by telephone. Many art collectors usually have a newly acquired piece of art reframed.

shop or a gallery. Working alongside more experienced framers is an excellent way to observe the craft and learn the finer points of framing.

Salary

Salaries for beginning picture framers are generally low. The PPFA reports that in 1999 most salaries fell between six and ten dollars an hour. A small number made fourteen dollars an hour and up.

Outlook

Skilled picture framers work in frame shops, art galleries, and museums. The majority of frame shops are mom-and-pop operations with one or two full- or part-time employees. If you are at the front counter, you should be a people person with math, art, and design skills. Workers in the back room must be organized, detail oriented, good at math, and able to do clean and accurate work.

If you decide to open your own picture framing business, consider building part of your customer base by establishing relationships with people in the arts and crafts community. If local artists and craftspeople are pleased with your work, your business will expand when they recommend you to their friends and associates. You may also want to stock your shop with framed prints and decorating accessories for added sales.

FOR MORE INFORMATION

ORGANIZATIONS

Art & Framing Council
501 Maggiore Court
Brentwood, CA 94513
(925) 516-0313
e-mail: info@artandframingcouncil.org
Web site: http://www.artandframingcouncil.org
This not-for-profit organization focuses on raising awareness about the art of custom framing. Members include publishers, art dealers, importers, manufacturers, and frame retailers.

Professional Picture Framers Association (PPFA)
4305 Sarellen Road
Richmond, VA 23231
(800) 556-6228
(804) 226-0430
Web site: http://www.ppfa.com
The largest trade organization for the industry, the PPFA membership includes more than 4,000 custom framers, art galleries, manufacturers, and distributors. The association provides its international members with up-to-date workshops as well as technical and marketing support.

SCHOOLS

American Picture Framing Academy
(888) 840-9605
Web site: http://www.pictureframingschool.com
The school's five-day courses and weekend programs teach custom framing procedures and techniques. Branches are located in Las Vegas, Nevada, and Southington, Connecticut.

Canadian Picture Framers School
Unit #1 - 20678 Duncan Way
Langley, BC V3A 7A3
Canada
(604) 533-5328
(888) 252-0040
Web site: http://www.framing-school.com

International Picture Framers School, Inc.
1128 Clyde Court
Kingston, ON K7P 2E4
Canada
(800) 294-0098
(705) 725-1250
Web site: http://www.framingschool.com
Basic and advanced classes for ten or fewer students per class.

New England Framing Academy
P.O. Box 814, King Court
Keene, NH 03431
(877) 797-6944
e-mail: dstretch@frameschool.com
Web site: http://www.frameschool.com
Using state-of-the-art equipment, students can learn to become professional picture framers. Workstations are supplied with professional mat cutters, joining vises, and hand tools.

WEB SITES

The International Institute for Frame Study (IIFS)
http://www.iifs.org
This is first public archive devoted to the history of picture frames. Curators, collectors, artisans, and frame enthusiasts will benefit from the information posted on this Web site.

Picture-Framer.com
http://www.picture-framer.com
Information for professional picture framers.

PERIODICALS

Picture Framing
P.O. Box 420
225 Gordons Corner Road
Manalapan, NJ 07726
(732) 446-4900
Web site: http://www.pictureframingmagazine.com
The only magazine devoted to the needs of professional picture framers. According to the Web site, "Our commitment to the growth and advancement of the framing industry has earned us the honor and responsibility of being the leading publication for the trade."

Southeastern Framer
P.O. Box 510
Acworth, GA 30101
(888) 388-7827
(770) 917-0710
e-mail: framer@go-star.com
Web site: http://www.go-star.com/framer
Up-to-the-minute industry news for frame shops and art galleries in the southeastern United States.

11

QUILT MAKER

With materials scarce in the American colonies, women recycled old clothes and sewing scraps into new and much-needed patchwork bedcovers. Early American patchwork patterns that became popular were given names such as Log Cabin, Double Wedding Ring, and Bear's Paw.

In the years before the American Civil War, people active with the

Underground Railroad hung patchwork quilts on outdoor lines with patterns that had specific meanings to help slaves escape safely to freedom.

Long considered mundane "women's work," over the last few decades patchwork quilts have earned the status of being one of America's great art forms. Today, as magnificent, historic patchwork quilts hang in the country's finest museums, we use newly stitched patchwork quilts to add visual warmth and beauty to our homes.

Description

A patchwork quilt is made of three layers. The top piece is a colorful composition of patchwork squares that have been assembled from many small pieces of cotton. The middle layer is large piece of cotton or synthetic quilt filling, and the bottom layer is a large sheet or plain fabric that has been stitched into a bigger, quilt-sized piece. The act of stitching together the three layers with delicate stitches is called quilting. When the layers are quilted together, they make a coverlet that is stronger, warmer, and much more attractive than any of the pieces would be alone.

Many quilt makers have set aside space in their homes just for their work. While professional quilt makers usually work alone, others work in cooperatives. Rarely do they work for companies.

Women have long helped each other "set" the tiny stitches that complete a quilt. When many women work together, the activity is called a quilting bee.

Patience is an important quality for quilt makers, even for those who sew together patchwork pieces by machine instead of by hand. In addition to having sewing skills, a quilt maker also needs a keen eye. A quilt maker needs to be organized, creative, and neat, with a flair for putting together fabrics and colors.

Education and Training

While quilt making is popular throughout the United States, Bob Ruggiero, publications manager at Quilts, Inc., part of the International Quilt Association, says, "We've found that the

Midwest is a real hotbed of quilting, along with areas of the Southeast and eastern seaboard." Many communities have local quilt shops where quilters can buy fabrics and other supplies. These shops are usually a hive of activity, where quilt makers can share ideas and take a variety of classes. Some classes are geared to beginners while others are tailored to people who have been stitching up storms for years.

"There is also a large network of traveling teachers who go to cities, sort of like 'quilting rock stars.' Large shows, like international quilt festivals, also give people an opportunity to meet big names in the industry, show their work, take classes, and network," says Ruggiero.

"For beginners," says Elaine Van Dusen of Quilts by Elaine, "I strongly suggest starting with a very small project. Many fabric stores want students to start with bed quilts, but this is definitely not the way to go. Beginners will be overwhelmed and never finish. You want to see results sooner than that." Ruggiero adds, "The most important way to learn is to just quilt, quilt, quilt!"

Salary

According to Ruggiero, "Quilts can sell from the $100 to $200 range to upwards of $20,000 to $40,000." Prices depend on factors such as design, intricacy, craftsmanship, quilt size, materials, and the reputation of the quilter. There is no set salary for quilters.

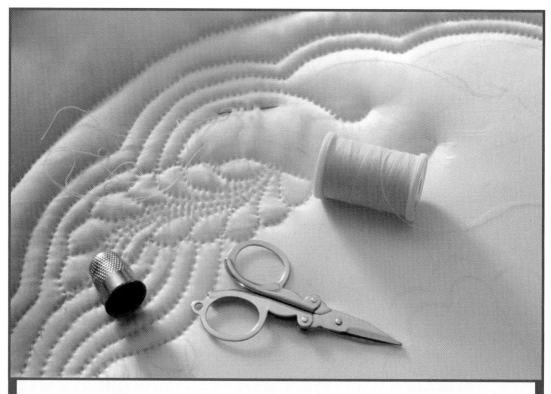

With a technique called trapunto, the quilter uses the running stitch and padded filling to create a design in high relief.

Outlook

Quilt makers can earn money by working on private commissions, selling their work through craft shops, shows, and galleries, and entering quilt competitions. Many quilt makers supplement their income by quilting other people's quilt tops, teaching, lecturing, writing books, and creating patterns and products. Quilters who specialize in making quilts for babies sometimes get commissions through children's specialty stores.

Ask fellow artists how the market is in your area. And be sure to register with your state for a tax resale number, which will enable you to buy supplies wholesale.

"While the vast majority of quilt makers are hobbyists, a section do make their living as full-time quilt makers who either work on commission, live off their prize money, or have their works hanging in museums and art galleries," reports Bob Ruggiero.

The cost of opening a store is very expensive and many small businesses don't survive because of overhead. If your financial resources are limited, consider finding work in a quilting or fabric store where you can help other quilt makers with their creations or give lessons. You might also run quilt making classes at home, or teach quilt making in community programs.

Getting Started with Quilt Making

Elaine Van Dusen of Quilts by Elaine (http://www. quiltsbyelaine.com) was a nurse when she first discovered quilt making. "I was working in a coronary care unit at a local hospital and spotted an ad for a quilting class in the paper. As soon as the class was underway, I knew this was something I would love doing and that it would be a great stress releaser," she reported.

"It wasn't long after I left CCU that my mother, who suffered from Alzheimer's disease, came to live with us. My free time to take classes was limited so I kept buying books and trying new things. I am mostly self-taught."

Before trying to make your first quilt, Van Dusen strongly advises "taking a few good classes to learn the basics. Then you can try different processes and patterns on your own. Small classes with no more than eight people work very well and allow for that added help that is often needed."

Once you've learned the basics, you'll be able to choose a specialty. Although she makes many different types of quilts, Van Dusen says, "I really like doing patchwork. I can do appliqué [the technique of stitching a fabric shape on top of a fabric square] but don't care for it. I taught myself hand quilting, so I often spend evenings doing that while sitting with my husband watching TV."

Van Dusen now works from her home in Jeffersonville, Vermont, and has expanded her business. "I started in one room in my house and over the past twelve years have added three more. I rise every morning at 6 AM and, because of my Web site, I spend about two hours on the computer. I start working at 9:30 and work until 4:30," she says. Van Dusen has cut back on her business hours to allow for more time to make quilts. Her shop is open four days a week, and on other days by appointment. "I love the independence and being responsible for making my business work," she reports.

As an experienced quilt maker and small-business owner, Van Dusen certainly knows some of the best ways to get started. "You can start out by doing local crafts shows that charge to rent a table, so the cost is very low," she says. "It takes time for your work to get known, but joining your local chamber of commerce is very helpful." Van Dusen suggests that when you are ready to turn your quilt making into a business, contact your local SCORE organization, which offers free advice and counseling. SCORE is made up of retired businesspeople who can answer all sorts of questions and give outstanding advice. SCORE stands for Service Corps of Retired Executives.

Another great source recommended by Van Dusen is the Small Business Bureau, which offers extremely help-ful advice. A business course can be really useful, so check local schools or community colleges for classes.

FOR MORE INFORMATION

ORGANIZATIONS

The Appliqué Society
P.O. Box 1030
Langley, WA 98260-1030
(800) 597-9827
Web site: http://www.theappliquesociety.org
This nonprofit organization is devoted to the art of appliqué. Members include artists, teachers, designers, writers, collectors, and other appliqué enthusiasts.

American Quilter's Society
P.O. Box 3290
Paducah, KY 42002-3290
(270) 898-7903
e-mail: info@aqsquilt.com
Web site: http://www.aqsquilt.com
Amateur and professional quilters, collectors, and quilt enthusiasts make up the 50,000 members of this group.

Canadian Quilters' Association
Carol Cooney, Membership Director
Box 24
Armstrong, BC V0E 1B0
Canada
(877) 672-8777
e-mail: pcooney@junction.net
Web site: http://www.canadianquilter.com/index.html
The goals of this association include promoting understanding and appreciation of patchwork, appliqué, and quilting.

International Quilt Association

7660 Woodway Drive, Suite 550
Houston, TX 77063
(713) 781-6864
e-mail: iqa@quilts.com
Web site: http://www.quilts.org
This nonprofit organization is dedicated to bring together from around the world quilt makers, quilt collectors, quilting teachers, retailers, and suppliers. Offering continuing education and support for the developing needs of quilters, it seeks to encourage the art and appreciation of quilts.

Mountain Cabin Quilters Guild

Box 8008
Canmore, AB T1W 2T8
Canada
Web site: http://www.diversitymetrics.com/quilt
This guild enables quilters to meet and share quilting activities. It offers classes and quilt exhibits.

National Quilting Association, Inc. (NQA)

P.O. Box 393
Ellicott City, MD 21041-0393
(410) 461-5733
Web site: http://www.nqaquilts.org
With approximately 5,500 members and more than 200 active chapters in 33 states, this association is concerned with the education of quilters and of the quilting community.

BOOKS

Bonsib, Sandy. *Flannel Quilts*. Woodinville, WA: Martingale & Co., 2001.

De Koning-Stapel, Hanne Vibeke. *Silk Quilts: From the Silk Road to the Quilter's Studio*. Lincolnwood, IL: NTC/Contemporary Publishing Group, 2000.

Ehrlich, Laura. *Complete Idiots Guide to Quilting*. New York: Simon & Schuster Macmillan Co., 1998.

Gordon, Maggi McCormick. *Pictorial Quilting.* New York: Watson-Guptill Publications, 2000.

Rymer, Cyndy Lyle. *Quilts for Guys: 15 Fun Projects for Your Favorite Fella*. Concord, CA: C & T Publishing, 2001.

PERIODICALS

The Quilter Magazine
All American Crafts, Inc.
243 Newton-Sparta Road
Newton, NJ 07860
(973) 383-8080
Web site: http://www.thequiltermag.com

12

STAINED GLASSMAKER

Do you have what it takes to become a stained glass craftsperson? Patience is especially valuable, but you must also be skilled with tools, and be committed to studying art and art history.

Many stained glass artists create windows for religious buildings. To be successful, it is important that a stained

A stained glass artist works on a project inside her studio. Stained glass artists are often contracted to create windows for religious institutions, colleges, and museums.

glass artist understand and respect religions and the needs of each congregation.

Description

The art of stained glass involves creating a design that will be pieced together from many small pieces of colorful glass. Stained glass as we know it today was first created about a thousand years ago for religious windows in Europe. At that time, the clear glass was colored with a stain.

Eventually, glassmakers were able to incorporate color into the glass by adding minerals and metals to hot glass. People who work in the medium of stained glass today don't necessarily make the glass themselves. Often, the glass is already made and ready for the stained glass artist to use. Cathedral glass, made by machine, is available in a variety of textures. Opalescent glass has a milky or marbleized appearance. Overlaying a layer of colored glass with frosted, clear, or amber glass creates an effect called flashed glass.

Glass can be etched or sandblasted to remove its outer layer, creating a design by revealing the layer below. While stained glass is most commonly associated with windows, other products made from stained glass include wall decorations, lamps, sun catchers (panels that are placed over windows), and ornaments. When illuminated from behind by light, stained glass adds a soft glow of color to a room.

Education and Training

With a learning process that is long and time consuming, it takes much practice and patience to become a skilled stained glass artist. "Most of the training for stained glass comes from being on the job with major studios," says Richard Gross of the *Stained Glass Quarterly*, published by

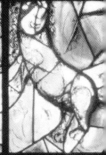

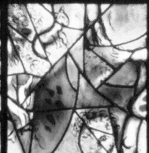

The stained glass window at the United Nations includes several symbols of peace and love as well as musical images. It was designed by French artist Marc Chagall.

How a Stained Glass Panel is Made

A design for stained glass windows begins as a full-size cartoon, or preparatory drawing on paper. Sometimes the craftsperson draws the cartoon. Other times the cartoon is supplied by a customer or an outside designer.

Colored glass is selected based on the cartoon and purpose of the window. Then the glass is cut with a glasscutter to fit the shapes depicted in the cartoon. Smooth-jawed pliers are used to cut the glass into shapes that have awkward curves.

To apply a design to glass, an artist uses a mixture of powdered glass and metal oxides that becomes a black or brown paint when water is added. The artist carefully traces the lines from the cartoon onto the glass. To achieve a shaded effect, the stained glassmaker uses a thinner wash, which is left on the glass to dry. When it is ready to be fired, the glass is loaded into the upper part of a kiln. The temperature of the kiln fuses the paint to the glass. Because of the high temperature, the glass becomes strained, so it's necessary to leave the glass in the kiln to cool slowly.

Lead is used to edge each piece of glass because it provides a strong, flexible bond. The lead is cut and bent in order to match the contours of each piece. The glass, surrounded by lead, is fused together.

the Stained Glass Association of America (SGAA, http://www.stainedglass.org). However, Gross adds that this is especially true in the area of architectural stained glass. Most stained glass is made for religious institutions. "While most studios no longer have official apprenticeship programs," he says, "they do, of course, train people to do the work of stained glass."

There are many stained glass studios that employ between five and twenty people. "I would definitely recommend beginning a stained glass career at one of these larger studios," says Gross. He also suggests taking classes taught in other educational settings, such as craft schools or adult education workshops.

Another way to learn about stained glass is by reading books. Gross points out that "books that approach stained glass as a craft with a long history and cover stained glass in an architectural context are useful."

Salary

The salary for stained glass artisans varies according to their experience and the quality of their work. "Someone who is accomplished in the field will make a nice living. With some experience and talent, novices will begin to see a much nicer income, too," reports Gross.

Outlook

The future for work in stained glass is bright. "It has enjoyed 200 years of steady growth, and now that restoration is becoming more common in this country, that pattern of growth looks likely to continue," says Gross. The East Coast has always had a high demand, and with the need for restoration growing, that will continue. The West Coast market for stained glass is expanding, too. Each of the major cities of the Midwest support several studios.

"Stained glass can be a very frustrating field, but it can also be very rewarding," says Gross. "The stained glass artist's job is to create a product of the highest craftsmanship for a client with the highest expectations. Anything less than the best is a failure."

FOR MORE INFORMATION

ORGANIZATIONS

Art Glass Association
1100-H Brandywine Boulevard
P.O. Box 3388
Zanesville, OH 43702-3388
(740) 452-4541
e-mail: info@agsa.org
Web site: http://www.artglassassociation.com
This not-for-profit trade association promotes the interests of the art glass supplies and products industry. It provides educational opportunities to encourage the professional growth of its members.

Artists in Stained Glass (AISG)
Box 333
253 College Street
Toronto, ON M5T 1R5
Canada
Web site: http://www.aisg.on.ca
AISG is a "nonprofit association of artists, craftspeople, architects, and others who are interested in the development and promotion of stained glass as a contemporary art form."

Association of Stained Glass Lamp Artists (ASGLA)
5070 Cromwell Drive NW
Gig Harbor, WA 98335
Web site: http://www.asgla.com
Promoting the craft of stained glass lamp construction, ASGLA publishes a bimonthly newsletter.

Cedar Moon Glass Ltd.
15840-80A Avenue
Surrey, BC V3S 8B6
Canada
(604) 597-3821
(877) 544-0601
e-mail: info@cedarmoon.com
Web site: http://www.cedarmoon.com
A working art glass studio, they offer stained glass supplies, lessons, custom work, and specialty gift items.

The Stained Glass Association of America (SGAA)
10009 East 62nd Street
Raytown, MO 64133
(800) 888-SGAA (7422)
e-mail: sgaa@stainedglass.org
Web site: http://www.stainedglass.org
Offering guidelines and training, the SGAA seeks to advance understanding and appreciation of stained glass.

Stained Glass Warehouse, Inc.
P.O. Box 609
Arden, NC 28704-0609
(828) 650-0992
e-mail: info@stainedglasswarehouse.com
Web site: http://www.stainedglasswarehouse.com
Crafters will find here a large selections of stained glass, tools, and supplies.

WEB SITES

Stained Glass Facts
http://www.thestorefinder.com/glass.html
Well-known stained glass publisher Randy Wardell offers step-by-step instructions for creating stained glass. Wardell includes history and answers to frequently asked questions, as well as a list of stained glass publications and trade organizations.

Stained Glass Patterns

http://www.downeaststainedglass.com/freestainedglasspatterns.html
For inspiration and ideas about stained glass patterns you can create.

Stained Glass Resources

http://www.stainedglasscanada.com
This directory offers information to those seeking Canadian stained glass artists, studios, retailers, wholesale distributors, and organizations. Also included are stained glass bulletin board forums, Canadian stained glass auctions, and stained glass classified ads.

BOOKS

Isenberg, Anita. *How To Work in Stained Glass*. 3rd ed. Iola, WI: Krause Publications, 1998.

Wrigley, Lynette. *The Complete Stained Glass Course: How to Master Every Major Glass Work Technique, with Thirteen Stunning Projects to Create*. Edison, NJ: Chartwell Books, 1996.

WEAVER

For the ultra-patient artistic person with great manual dexterity and an eye for texture and color, weaving can be extremely rewarding. Beginning weavers should start with a small tabletop loom. Over time, as a weaver becomes more experienced, he or she can purchase or build a larger loom.

Description

Archaeologists believe that some form of weaving has been part of every developing civilization, although no one has been able to determine exactly where or when weaving began. Few early clues have survived. Primitive humans are likely to have woven together sticks and reeds for clothing, blankets, hammocks, rugs, pouches, and other containers.

To weave is to interlace two sets of threads. Today, rugs, table linens, wall hangings, and clothing are just some of the items that weavers create.

First the weaver attaches one set of threads, called the warp, lengthwise on a loom. The warp threads must be parallel and an equal distance from each other. The weaver guides the weft threads, or horizontal threads, over and under the warp threads, passing them crosswise—from one side of the warp to the other, and back again.

Before beginning work, many weavers prefer to sketch their designs and enlarge the drawing to the intended size. The weaver draws a grid over the first drawing, and then draws a grid on a larger sheet of paper with the same dimensions as the design. The weaver copies the squares from the smaller grid onto the larger grid in the corresponding area. This enlargement is called a cartoon. The cartoon is pinned behind the warp and traced with a marker. The weaver is then able to transfer the cartoon directly onto the loom.

A weaver maps out a pattern on a sketch grid for a Turkish rug.

Almost any kind of material can be woven. Wire, strips of fabric, leather, yarn, and even paper can be interlaced to form beautiful designs. From the materials and weaves, an artisan can create geometric, striped, and other kinds of patterns.

The plain weave, also called the tabby weave, is extremely simple. To do it, the craftsperson weaves the weft over and under the warp threads, making sure they alternate the pattern with each row. This type of weave may be done tightly or loosely depending on the material, the type of work the weaver is trying to produce, and the look he or she wants to achieve.

The basket weave follows a similar technique as the plain weave. With the basket weave, however, two warp threads are interlaced with two weft threads. When using two different colors, the result is a checkerboard pattern.

Education and Training

To become a weaver you should be extra patient because weaving can take a tremendous amount of time. Most weavers have rooms set up in their homes for weaving. Looms can be large, so it is a good idea to have a space that can accommodate them.

Weaver Jessica Speer advises people interested in weaving to take a class or two and to get in touch with the local weaver's guild, if there is one nearby. "Looms and the associated equipment are very expensive," says Speer, so she strongly suggests taking a class to make sure weaving is for you. "Anyone can learn, but not everyone enjoys it. If you aren't enjoying the process, you won't want to put the time and effort into it."

"I took two six-week classes at the local community college's outreach program," says Speer. "I was teamed up with an old friend who had been weaving for years and I learned as much from her as I did from the teacher." Eventually, Speer bought her own loom and began to weave at home.

The weaver must string the many needle eyes of the tapestry loom according to the constructed pattern. The warps, or vertical threads, form the base of the tapestry. The wefts, or horizontal threads, make the pattern.

Profile

Jessica Speer, a weaver from Wisconsin, has set up shop in her home. "I've always woven here at home," she says. "When I first started, I had the loom, sometimes two looms, in the second bedroom of my apartment. When I bought this house, I remodeled an attached shed into a studio." Her work tended to take over most of the house.

Her work hours, like those of many weavers, depend upon her projects. She doesn't have a set schedule. "I'm semi-retired now, so I work just a few hours a day," she

explains. "In the beginning, I often worked ten to twelve hours a day, six days a week, and sometimes Sundays, too. The hours for the self-employed are never really regular, and artists work when they get an idea. The whole thing plays havoc with your social and family life."

Salary

Weavers, like most craftspeople who are self-employed, do not have a standard of salary. The *Crafts Report*'s 1999 Insight Survey indicates that fiber artists earned an average of $14,492 a year. However, there are some

Advice from Jessica Speer, Weaver

"Designing takes an artistic person who knows the possibilities and limitations of the medium. And the business requires all the usual business skills and a marketing genius," says Speer. "I like designing and often have several things in mind while I have one on the loom. I least like, but do not dislike, just throwing the shuttle, with no more design work, which is why I'm moving to more figurative designs. Marketing is the most difficult part of the business, and the area I would love to hand off to someone else."

weavers who command hundreds or thousands of dollars for their work.

Speer offers these words of caution to people who expect to make a lot of money by weaving. "If you want to make a living doing this," she says, "you may very well be disappointed. If you really want to weave for sale, production work might be for you. If you can offer a wholesale line of many very similar pieces, you may have a market with upscale retailers. Small things that may be gifts sell better, but don't bring in the net profit that bigger things do."

Outlook

Most weavers sell their work through craft fairs and galleries or from their studios. Jessica Speer doesn't have a store. "Some of my work is in two relatively local galleries, some sells online, some sells by word of mouth, and some hasn't sold yet," she says. Weavers can also teach, sell weaving supplies, or write books and articles to supplement their incomes.

A few weavers earn large commissions to produce enormous compositions that will hang in public spaces such as hotels, office buildings, airports, or theaters. While some fiber artists even have their work hanging in museums, they are the exceptions.

FOR MORE INFORMATION

ORGANIZATIONS

Edmonton Weavers' Guild

Prince of Wales Armouries
10440 108 Avenue
Edmonton, AB T5H 3Z9
Canada
(780) 425-9280
Web site: http://www.freenet.edmonton.ab.ca/weavers
Members receive five issues of the newsletter, *Webs & Wheels*, and have access to their library, study groups, and studio. Members can also enter work in their annual show and sale.

Guild of Canadian Weavers

714 Hazell Road
Kelowna, BC V1W 1R3
Canada
e-mail: contact@the-gcw.org
Web site: http://www.the-gcw.org
Open to those interested in hand weaving.

Handweavers Guild of America, Inc. (HGA)

Two Executive Concourse, Suite 201
3327 Duluth Highway
Duluth, GA 30096-3301
(770) 495-7702
e-mail: weavespindye@compuserve.com
Web site: http://www.weavespindye.org
This is a nonprofit organization for weavers, spinners, dyers, basket makers, bead weavers, felters, and other fiber artists. Members receive a subscription to *Shuttle Spindle & Dyepot*.

Textile Society of America
P.O. Box 70
Earleville, MD 21919-0070
(410) 275-2329
e-mail: tsa@dol.net
Web site: http://textilesociety.org
A forum for the exchange of information about textiles, including the the history, the culture, the economics, and the techniques. With 500 members worldwide, membership includes museum curators, teachers, historians, artists, students, dealers, and collectors.

WEB SITES

About Weaving
http://www.weaving.about.com/hobbies/weaving
Articles and links to weaving and textile sites on the Internet.

Rugweavers' Workshop
http://www.rugweavers.com
Receive instruction on this site, which is dedicated to rug weaving. Expert ring weavers will answer your questions.

Weavers Hand
http://www.weavershand.com
Although specifically for tablet weaving, kumihimo, and ply-splitting, this site also features links to other weaving Web sites.

14

WOODWORKER

Crafting with wood is one area where the possibilities seem endless. For centuries, people have shaped wood by carving, cutting, or polishing. Wood is often used for home accessories, for furniture, and for sculpture because it can be made into such beautiful shapes and is so durable.

Description

While woodcarvers usually work by hand using tools such as chisels and knives, sometimes carvers use power tools. The woodcarvers who use machines can choose from chainsaws, jigsaws, and sanders, depending on the scale of their project. Sometimes the creations of woodcarvers are for decoration, and other times they are meant to be used. Woodcrafters may carve animals, statues, figures, and walking sticks, or they may construct cabinets, bookcases, tables, chairs, or doors.

Education and Training

Many high schools offer classes in woodworking. In addition, check the offerings at local adult education programs and colleges. If you are fortunate enough to know a woodworker in the particular area that interests you, ask to be an apprentice.

Woodcrafter Sue Jennings, who works with her husband, Stan, reports that "anyone can learn woodworking with time, patience, and a good teacher. They need to just keep at it. Stay focused on your goal and don't despair if things go slow." She adds, "If you are young, time is on your side.

Woodcrafters, especially those who create pieces that may be exposed to varying room temperatures or weather conditions, need to know the difference between the many types of wood.

A guitar maker uses a knife to shave the inside of a guitar's face.

We didn't start our business until we were almost middle aged and we wish we had started many years earlier."

Salary

According to the 1999 Insight Survey of the *Crafts Report*, people who work with wood earned an average of $24,819 per year. However, this figure varies according to the woodworking specialty. Years of experience and expertise also play a role in determining salary. A more skillful woodworker may charge more money than a person new to the field.

Outlook

Cabinetmakers hold many of the jobs in the woodworking industry. They specialize in building wood cabinets for homes and businesses. Other woodworking professionals may work in factories or workshops. Sometimes, cabinetmakers build cabinets at the site; other times, they build cabinets in their workspace and install them later. Cabinetmakers must be precise with their measurements and work. Cabinetmakers can express their more artistic sides when creating a design, choosing wood, or putting a finish on cabinets.

Woodturners shape, polish, and cut wood into decorative creations. They use equipment such as lathes to shave the wood into objects that can be anything from bowls and boxes to sculptures.

Guitar makers can work for companies that manufacture guitars, or they can craft guitars in their own workshops. Acoustic and electric guitars are usually made from rosewood, spruce, mahogany, or cedar.

Toy makers use wood to create toys that will last for years. Handcrafted toys often outlast their plastic counterparts and make unique gifts. Wooden toys are often the most popular items at craft fairs. A skilled woodworker might branch into toy making to expand his or her offerings.

Profile

Sue Jennings and her husband, Stan, did not start out as woodworkers. When they met in 1984, they were working underground in West Virginia's coal mines. The mines closed a year later, and, after several other types of jobs, Sue and Stan decided in 1990 to pursue a dream they both shared—woodworking. And so began their business, Allegheny Treenware (http://www.spooners.com).

Says Sue Jennings, "Our interest must have been born into us. My father was a contractor and Stan's was a sawmill operator. When we met we shared a dream of being wood-workers from the very beginning." Both are self-taught wood-workers, learning by what she calls "lots of trial and error."

The Jennings have received many honors at the craft fairs and festivals that they have attended over the years. In 1999, they were listed in the Early American Homes *annual directory of top 200 craftsmen. As a result, they received an invitation to create an ornament for the White House Christmas tree as well as an invitation to see the tree.*

These days they concentrate on making many different types of wooden spoons. "We made a lot of things to start with," reports Sue, "and we kept selling the spoons that we made. Before long we stopped doing everything else but them."

The Jennings workshop is located in their backyard in Preston County, West Virginia. Says Sue, "If we aren't eating or sleeping, we are in the shop working. We begin no later than 8:00 AM and leave the shop about 9:00 PM every day we are home."

They attend about twenty-three shows a year, which gives them a break from the shop. Sue says that "the best thing is meeting so many wonderful people—fellow artisans and the general public." And what she likes the least? "Being stuck at my desk doing paperwork and working on the computer, which I really don't understand but have to put up with."

For those who want to get started in woodworking, Sue thinks a good avenue would be to take your work to some sort of venue—perhaps a consignment shop or craft show—to sell it. "The more you practice your craft, the better you will become and the more likely your hobby will turn into a business."

FOR MORE INFORMATION

ORGANIZATIONS

Northwest Wood Carvers Association
P.O. Box 6092
Federal Way, WA 98063-6092
Web site: http://www.woodcarvers.org/index.htm
People interested in woodcarving as an art can improve their skills through instruction offered by this association. Activities are available to members.

The Pacific Woodworkers Guild
P.O. Box 63071
6020 Steveston Highway
Richmond, BC V7E 2K0
Canada
Web site: http://members.shaw.ca/pwwg/home.htm
British Columbians who are woodworking enthusiasts belong to this nonprofit guild.

SCHOOLS

The American Woodcarving School
21 Pompton Plains Crossroad
Wayne, NJ 07470
(973) 835-8555
Web site: http://www.americanwoodcarving.com

American Woodworking Academy, Inc.
1495 Hoff Industrial Drive
O'Fallon, MO 63366-2336
(636) 240-1804
e-mail: info@awacademy.com
Web site: http://www.awacademy.com

WEB SITES

Amateur Woodworker
http://www.am-wood.com
Amateur Woodworker, published eleven times a year, is the only magazine aimed at wookworking hobbyists. it is available at no cost on the Internet.

Better Woodworking
http://www.betterwoodworking.com/associations.htm
Online woodworking information.

PERIODICALS

Canadian Woodworking
RR #3
Burford, ON N0E 1A0
Canada
e-mail: fulcher@canadianwoodworking.com
Web site: http://www.canadianwoodworking.com/aboutus.php
Dedicated to woodworking, this national magazine is for people of all skill levels, from the hobbyist to the advanced woodworker. It features plans, projects, tips, tool reviews, coming events, and book and video reviews. It also includes information on woodturning, woodcarving, intarsia, scroll saw, router, marquetry cabinetry, and more.

Creative Woodworks and Crafts
All American Crafts, Inc.
243 Newton-Sparta Road
Newton, NJ 07860
(973) 383-8080

Popular Woodworking
F&W Publications, Inc.
4700 East Galbraith Road
Cincinnati, OH 45236
Web site: http://www.popularwoodworking.com
In each issue, you will find plans for projects, tool reviews, and in-depth articles on woodworking techniques for the beginning, intermediate, and expert woodworker.

Woodworker's Journal
P.O. Box 56585
Boulder, CO 80322-6585
(800) 765-4119
Web site: http://www.woodworkersjournal.com/index.cfm
This journal includes plans to build great projects, reviews of woodworking tools, and lots of woodworking tips and techniques.

GLOSSARY

abstract The representation of an image or idea with unfamiliar symbols or marks.

adhere To stick or cling.

apprentice A person who works under a skilled craftsperson to learn a trade.

congregation An assembly of people for religious worship.

consignment shop A store that pays the supplier of an item after it sells.

consistency Firmness or thickness; the condition of holding together.

contemporary Modern; present-day.

crucible A heat-resistant container used for melting ores and metals.

dictate To command expressly.

distinctive Having a special style.

distinguished Noted for excellence.

durability Able to last for a long time without deterioration.

embellish To decorate or adorn.

essential Necessary or indispensable.

ethical Conforming to moral or professional codes of behavior or conduct.

guild An association or group formed for the aid and promotion of common interests.

heirloom A possession handed down from generation to generation.

kiln A furnace or oven used for baking or firing pottery or ceramics.

loom A frame or machine for weaving thread or yarn to form cloth.

marketing Promoting a product or service.

metropolitan An area in or near a large city.

modular Constructed with standardized units.

novice A person new to a particular activity.

primitive Crude or simple.

porous Full of holes, or pores, through which light, air, or fluids can pass.

recruit To enlist new members into an organization.

retail Goods sold in small quantities directly to a customer.

scale Size or proportion.

sentimental Evoking a feeling or emotion rather than reason.

significance Being meaningful or important.

spindle A rod that revolves or serves as an axis for a revolving part.

standards Rules or regulations.

supplement To add; to make up for a lack of something else.

symmetrical Correspondence of parts in shape, size, and position. One half is a mirror reflection of the other.

tactile Perceived or understood by the sense of touch.

tenacity The quality of not being easy to pull apart. Holding tight; to put up with; to endure.

tradition Belief, custom, or style handed down from generation to generation.

translucent The condition of letting some light pass through, but not being completely clear.

unobtrusive Not bold; inconspicuous.

vocational Relating to a career or trade.

wholesale Goods sold in large quantities to retailers.

INDEX

About the Author

Stephanie Mannino is a freelance writer living in Chatham, New Jersey.

Acknowledgements

The author would like to thank the following people for taking the time to share their knowledge and expertise in their chosen field of crafting: Wayne Christensen, Sharon Dugan, Denis Gouey, Richard Gross, Sue Jennings, Janelle Johnson, Thom Keach, Linda Powers, Ron Ross, Bob Ruggiero, Jessica Speer, Richard Tuttle, Elaine Van Dusen, and Mary M. Wiseman.

Photo Credits

Cover © Stuart Cohen/The Image Works; pp. 10, 12 © Michael J. Doolittle/The Image Works; pp. 14, 40, 96, 98 © Syracuse Newspapers/The Image Works; pp. 19, 20 © Michael Freeman/Corbis; p. 23 © Owen Franken/Corbis; pp. 29, 30 © Phil Schermeister/Corbis; pp. 37, 38 © Cameron Yarborough/*San Angelo Standard-Times*/AP/ Wide World Photos; pp. 45, 46 © Brett Butterstein/*The Daily Times*/AP/Wide World Photos; p. 48 © Robert Borea/ AP/Wide World Photos; pp. 54, 55 © Dave Bartruff/Index Stock Imagery; p. 58 © Michael S. Yamashita/Corbis;

Editor

Jill Jarnow

Design and Layout

Evelyn Horovicz